Cool Kids Cook

For Donna's nieces (who we love to pieces) Elisha + Gabrielle, Ness + Simon's beautiful new baby and Dan's wild child, Duke. Thanks and love to our big kids, too—Bill, Simon and John—for letting us play together on the weekends, and to our publisher, Catie Ziller, for leaving us to our own devices on this one, and trusting in the result.

Published in 2000 by Murdoch Books Pty Limited. Paperback edition first published in 2004.
Reprinted in 2005.

National Library of Australia Cataloging-in-Publication Data
Hay, Donna. Cool Kids Cook.
Inculdes index. ISBN 1 74045 548 7
1. Cookery - Juvenile literature. I. Holden, Danielle. II. Holden, Vanessa. III. Title.
641 5123

Text, illustrations and design © Donna Hay, Danielle Holden and Vanessa Holden 2000.

Original concept: Donna Hay, Danielle Holden and Vanessa Holden

Recipes: Donna Hay
Editor: Jane Price
Project Manager: Anna Waddington
Recipe Testing: Ben Masters, Briget Palmer

Art Director: Vanessa Holden
Illustrator: Danielle Holden
Designer: Anderson C S Mendes
Chief Executive: Juliet Rogers
Publisher: Kay Scarlett

Published in Australia by Murdoch Books Pty Limited Pier 8/9, 23 Hickson Road, Sydney, NSW 2000.
Phone: 61 (02) 8220 2000 Fax: 61 (02) 8220 2558
Published in UK by Murdoch Books Pty Limited Erico House, 6th Floor North, 93/99 Upper Richmond Road,
Putney, London, SW15 2TG. Phone: + 44 (0) 20 8785 5995 Fax: + 44 (0) 20 8785 5985

Printed by Tien Wah Press. PRINTED IN SINGAPORE.

Cool Kids Cook

Donna Hay

with illustrations by Danielle Holden

MURDOCH BOOKS

inside

savoury

sweet

get cooking...

Cooking is cool. It's fun to do with your friends and family, and it's fun to share the food you make as well. The recipes in this book show how easy it can be. Each recipe leads you step-by-step to a new taste sensation. Make it easy on yourself by taking the time to read the safety, tips and tools pages up the front: they are full of good ideas. Also, check the ingredients and tools lists at the beginning of each recipe to make sure you're absolutely ready to go. Sometimes you may have to ask a grown-up for help, but that's OK (they do come in handy every so often). People love to get together over food—enjoy sharing what you make and get ready for all the compliments!

Safety

The levels of difficulty vary from recipe to recipe. Parents are requested to supervise their children in the kitchen at all times.

Ovens & Cooktops

● Ovens and cooktops are serious stuff—they get very hot and can give you a very very nasty burn. Ask an older person to help you, so that you can sail through your recipe. Treat your oven like the school-yard bully—be careful.

● Always use oven mitts when taking things in and out of the oven—the door, sides and racks are hot as the oven is preheated.

● Use oven mitts that are small enough for your hands—large oven mitts may get in your way and make it harder to handle hot baking trays.

● Arrange the shelves in the oven before you turn on the oven to preheat it.

● If you use a wet tea towel to remove hot baking dishes from the oven, the heat will go straight through the tea towel and give you a nasty burn.

● It is best to put boiling pans at the back of the cooktop and never leave them unattended. Remember to turn off the oven or cooktop when you are finished.

● When you are plugging in your electric mixer, make sure your hands are dry. Check that the mixer is switched off at the dial before you turn on the power at the wall.

● Use a wire rack when cooling hot baking dishes so that you don't make scorch marks on the benchtop.

Knives & Chopping

● When cooking with a saucepan or frypan, turn the handle to the side of the cooktop so that nobody can knock it and tip the hot contents over themselves or you. Be sure you don't turn the handle towards another hot plate that is on or the handle will heat up and give you a bad burn when you try to pick up the pan.

● When opening the oven door, stand back so that the hot steam can escape before you remove your hot baking tray. Always wear your oven mitts and be sure that your path is clear before removing something from the oven to the benchtop.

● Wear an apron to protect your clothes and skin from any cooking splatters. Keep it tied around you, especially when you are working at the cooktop or oven.

● If you are not experienced or big enough, ask an older person to do all the chopping required for the recipe. That way you'll avoid accidents with the knife.

● If you are chopping with a knife, always use a chopping board and be sure that the chopping board doesn't slip on your bench. If it does slip, put a damp tea towel underneath to keep it steady. Always wash the board and knife regularly between chopping raw meat products and fresh foods like vegetables or herbs.

● Remember not to put knives in the sink, especially when it is filled with water and suds. Somebody could reach in and give themselves a painful cut.

● Never cook in bare feet or open-toed shoes as a knife could drop or something hot could easily spill on your feet.

● When chopping something round like an onion or tomato, cut it in half first then put the cut side down on the chopping board so that you have a flat surface to cut on. It's easier and safer.

● If you are not confident chopping with a knife, roughly grate a peeled onion or carrot instead of chopping it.

and last but not least...

● If you spill something, clean it up before you slip in it—oops!

Tips

Getting things organised makes cooking a lot easier—here are some time-saving ideas

- Read the recipe all the way through before you start so that you are sure you have all the ingredients and tools. Set out the ingredients on the work surface so that they are within reach when you need them. Have them weighed out and prepared before you start.
- Preheat the oven before you start to cook so that it will have reached the right temperature by the time you are ready to use it.
- Clean up as you go along, otherwise you'll have a big pile of washing-up at the end. It is also safer to keep things tidy and out of your way.
- Measure liquids in a special jug and dry ingredients, such as flour and cocoa powder, in measuring cups.
- When you are measuring, make sure you fill to the top of the line you are measuring to—not under or over. When using cups to measure dry ingredients, smooth the top of the contents with a knife to make them level for an accurate measure.
- Sift dry ingredients, such as flour and cocoa powder, to remove any lumps before you add them to mixing bowls.
- When you are cooking, set a timer. When the buzzer goes off you know that your cooking time has finished.
- Spills should be cleaned up as soon as they are made. Spills on the floor are slippery, so wipe them up with paper towels. On the work surface, use a sponge.
- Wash fruit and vegetables before you cook them. Mushrooms just need a wipe with a damp piece of paper towel. Don't rinse them or they'll go soggy.
- Refrigerate fresh meat or chicken in a bowl loosely covered with plastic wrap. It will keep for 3 days like this.
- Before icing a cake or cup-cakes, make sure that the cake is cold. If it is warm, the icing or cream will run straight off.
- Some ingredients in recipes are 'optional'. This means if you don't like something (like chilli sauce) you can make the recipe anyway.

Tools

Choosing the right tool for the job saves time and energy. Here's a quick rundown on some of the tools you'll be using.

Measuring jugs

Are for measuring liquids like stock, milk and cream. Bend down and have your eyes level with the line on the jug for an exact measure. Measure level to the top of the line—not under or over. A good measurer is a good cook.

Measuring cups

Come in 1-cup, 1/2-cup, 1/3-cup and 1/4-cup measures. A 1-cup measure holds 250 ml (8 fl oz). The cups are for measuring solids like rice, flour, cocoa powder, biscuit crumbs and sugar. To measure properly, heap the ingredient up over the top of the cup. Then use a knife or spatula to sweep over the top and make it level. This is important when baking cakes and biscuits.

Measuring spoons

Come in 1 tablespoon, 1 teaspoon, 1/2 teaspoon and 1/4 teaspoon measures. They are for measuring small amounts, like milk, baking powder and honey. With dry ingredients, heap them over the top, then use a knife or spatula to sweep over the top to make it level. This will give you an exact measure.

Kitchen scales

Are handy for weighing ingredients that are hard to measure accurately in cups—like chopped chocolate. The measure should be on zero to start, so put the bowl on first, then fill it with the ingredients.

Chopping board

Use a wooden or hard plastic board that is flat and clean. Always scrub clean when finished.

Knives

Are best kept sharp as less pressure is needed to cut. When you use less pressure, you are less likely to slip and cut yourself.

Saucepans

Have a set of saucepans in varying sizes. Small saucepans are good for melting butter or chocolate. Larger pans are great for boiling rice or pasta, or even making soup. They should have tight-fitting lids and solid handles that don't heat up when you are cooking in them.

Frypans

Are used to cook lots of foods. If you want to cook a stir-fry type of recipe like Chop Chop Suey (page 46), then a deep frypan with high sides is better so things don't splash over the sides. Non-stick frypans are great because you can cook without oil and they are easy to clean. Always use one with a steady solid handle that doesn't heat up when you cook in it.

Wok

Is a deep round frypan that is mainly used in Asian cooking. It is the perfect shape to toss all the ingredients around for a stir-fry. If you don't have a wok, you can use a deep frypan instead.

Stirring spoons

Can be either metal or wooden. When cooking curries, use a metal spoon as a wooden one will absorb the curry taste and may spoil your next cake mix.

Heatproof dish

Can be any dish that can stand the heat of the oven without cracking. If you are unsure, ask an older person or use a metal dish.

Baking trays

Are metal trays for cooking in the oven. The deep ones are for cooking things like Roast Chicken Dinner (page 53) and Gringo's Nachos (page 25), while the flat ones are for biscuits and cookies.

Colander

A colander with wide holes is used to drain pasta and boiled vegetables like potatoes. When you are draining hot things, the safest way is to place the colander in the sink and pour the hot contents into it. Be very careful and watch out for the steam as it rises.

Tools

Can opener

Makes opening cans a breeze. Use a can opener that takes the top off inside the edge so that there is not a sharp exposed edge left behind. Always be careful to avoid nicks and cuts from the lid as the opener cuts through.

Grater

Is a kitchen essential for grating cheese and vegetables like carrots and potatoes.

Egg flip

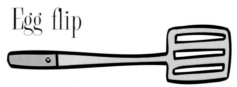

Is handy for turning things over in pans, or lifting them out, and not just eggs. It's a large flat spatula-type tool with a long handle so that you can pick up difficult things, such as fried eggs or pieces of pie.

Electric mixer

Makes cake-making easy. You may need the help of an older person to assemble the mixer and help you operate it. When making a cake, use the attachments that look like small whisks. If the mixer comes with a bowl, then use it. If it doesn't, then use a stable mixing bowl instead.

Mixing bowls

Use a bowl big enough to stir all the ingredients without them splashing over the sides. Metal or plastic bowls are great. Glass mixing bowls can be heavy—be careful not to drop them. A set of three mixing bowls is a good idea—small, medium and large.

Sieve

A fine mesh sieve is used to sift dry ingredients like flour and cocoa to remove any lumps and ensure your cake mixture is airy and smooth.

Spatula

This is great for scraping bowls or spreading fillings or icings over cakes. Big wide spatulas are also good for lifting pieces of pie from baking dishes onto serving plates.

Cake tins

Come in lots of sizes and shapes—round, square and rectangular. You can write the sizes on the undersides of the tins so that you don't have to measure them every time.

Non-stick baking paper

Is available in the supermarket. It comes in a roll and is lightly coated in silicon so that biscuits, cakes and any other cooked foods won't stick to the paper or the baking tray or tin. Using non-stick baking paper also makes washing-up easy.

Skewers

Use a metal or wooden skewer to poke into the middle of a cake to see if it is cooked. If the skewer comes out clean, then the cake is cooked. If the skewer comes out with wet mixture on it, then the cake needs more cooking time.

Cookie cutters

Come in lots of different shapes—stars, circles and gingerbread men. These are great for making Spaceman Eggs (page 17) or Strawberry & Cream Stars (page 93).

Wire racks

Are for cooling cakes or biscuits. It is best to cool biscuits on wire racks so that they turn crisp and not soggy. Wire racks are also great for putting hot dishes and pans on so that you don't scorch the benchtop.

Pastry brush

Is a handy tool for brushing pastry with melted butter or milk before cooking so that the pastry top turns golden. A pastry brush is also useful for brushing marinade on steaks, kebabs and chicken. Wash it well after use and let it dry on a window sill before you put it away.

Simple conversions

1 cup butter = 250 g
1 cup flour = 125 g
1 cup sugar = 250 g
1 cup caster sugar = 220 g
1 cup icing sugar = 155 g
1 cup rolled oats = 90 g

Spaceman Eggs

Yummy buttered toast blasts off into space with a runny, gooey, eggy centre

ingredients

2 slices bread
1 tablespoon butter
2 small eggs

tools

gingerbread man cookie cutter
frypan
spatula or egg flip
cup

Use the cookie cutter to cut a man shape from the middle of each slice of bread. If you don't have a man-shaped cookie cutter, a star or round shape will do.

Heat the butter in a frypan over medium heat and wait for it to melt. Place both slices of bread in the pan and cook until they are golden underneath. Turn the bread over with the spatula so that the golden side is on top.

Crack one of the eggs into a cup and then pour it into the man shape in one of the slices of bread. Do the same with the other egg and slice of bread. Cook for 4 minutes, or until the egg is cooked the way you like it. Serves 2

Jungle Curry

Feel the beat of the jungle in your mouth with this fiery (as you like) curry

ingredients

1 tablespoon oil
1 onion, chopped
2 teaspoons red curry paste
2 1/2 cups (20 fl oz) coconut milk
4 chicken breast fillets, sliced

1 red capsicum (pepper),
 chopped
1 cup chopped greens, such as
 beans or broccoli
rice or noodles, to serve

tools

knife + chopping board
measuring jug, cups + spoons
frypan
stirring spoon

Heat the oil in a large frypan over medium-high heat. Add the onion and cook, stirring, for 3 minutes, or until the onion is soft.

Add the curry paste and cook for 1 minute. Add the coconut milk to the pan and let it simmer for 5 minutes.

Add the chicken, capsicum and greens and let the curry simmer for 5 minutes, or until the chicken is cooked. Serve with rice or noodles.
Serves 4

Tip For a milder curry add less curry paste—for more fire just add more

Chicken Noodle Soup

Oodles of noodles and yummy chicken will make this soup a family favourite

ingredients

6 cups (48 fl oz) chicken stock
3 chicken breast fillets, chopped
150 g (5 oz) instant noodles
salt and pepper
chopped parsley, optional

tools

measuring jug
knife + chopping board
saucepan
stirring spoon
ladle

Place the chicken stock in a saucepan over high heat and wait for it to boil.

Add the chicken and stir so that the pieces don't stick together. Let the chicken cook in the stock for 4 minutes.

Add the noodles to the saucepan with a little salt and pepper and cook for 3 minutes, or until the noodles are soft. Ladle into bowls and sprinkle with parsley, if you like.
Serves 4

Mountains O'Macaroni

When things turn chilly, warm up with mountains of creamy cheesy pasta

ingredients

1 1/2 cups macaroni
1/2 cup (4 fl oz) cream
1/2 cup grated cheddar cheese

tools

measuring jug + cups
grater
saucepan
colander
stirring spoon

Place a saucepan of water over medium-high heat and wait until it boils. Add the macaroni and cook for 8 minutes, or until the macaroni is soft.

Drain the macaroni in a colander and then put it back into the saucepan. Turn the heat to low and put the pan back on the heat.

Add the cream and cheese to the macaroni and stir until the cheese has melted and the macaroni cheese is thick. Spoon into bowls to serve. Serves 2

Gringo's Nachos

Round up your gringos to help make and share this spicy Mexican favourite

ingredients

200 g (6 ½ oz) packet corn chips
2 cups grated cheddar cheese
2 tomatoes, chopped
4 spring (green) onions, chopped
2 tablespoons mild chilli sauce
375 g (12 oz) can red kidney
    beans, rinsed
chopped avocado, to serve

tools

grater
measuring cups + spoons
knife + chopping board
can opener
sieve
deep baking tray + oven mitts
bowl
stirring spoon + egg flip

Preheat the oven to 180°C (350°F/Gas 4). Place the corn chips in a deep baking tray and sprinkle with half the cheese.

In a bowl, mix together the tomatoes, onions, chilli sauce and beans. Spoon the mixture over the corn chips, then sprinkle with the rest of the cheese.

Bake in the oven for 25 minutes. Scoop out the nachos and serve with chopped avocado or guacamole (page 54), if you like. Serves 4

Spaghetti Bolognese

Give your tastebuds a treat—take them to Italy for the night

ingredients

2 teaspoons oil
1 onion, chopped
500 g (1 lb) minced (ground) beef
425 g (14 oz) tomato pasta
  sauce or canned tomato purée
400 g (13 oz) spaghetti

tools

measuring spoon
knife + chopping board
frypan
stirring spoon
saucepan
colander

Heat the oil in a large frypan over medium-high heat. Add the onion and cook for 4 minutes, or until the onion is soft. Add the minced beef and cook, stirring, for 5 minutes, or until the meat is brown.

Add the tomato purée and leave the sauce to simmer for 10 minutes, or until it has thickened.

While the bolognese sauce is simmering, cook the spaghetti in a large saucepan of boiling water for 10 minutes, or until it is soft. Drain the spaghetti in a colander and pile into serving bowls.
Top with the bolognese sauce.
Serves 4

Shepherds Pie

A double flavour whammy of meaty sauce and creamy potato packed into a pie

ingredients

1 quantity bolognese sauce (page 26)
4 large potatoes, peeled and
  chopped
1/3 cup (2 3/4 fl oz) milk
2 tablespoons butter
1 cup grated cheddar cheese

tools

vegetable peeler
knife + chopping board
measuring jug, cups + spoons
grater
heatproof dish
saucepan

colander
bowl
potato masher
large spoon
oven mitts

Make the bolognese sauce
(without the spaghetti) and pour
it into a heatproof dish. Preheat
the oven to 180°C (350°F/Gas 4).

Cook the potatoes in a large
saucepan of boiling water for
8 minutes, or until they are soft.
Drain the potatoes in a colander
and then place them in a bowl.
Add the milk, butter and half the
cheese and mash with a potato
masher until smooth.

Pile the potato on top of the
bolognese sauce and sprinkle
with the rest of the cheese.
Bake in the oven for 25 minutes,
or until the cheese on top is brown.
Serves 6

Tex Mex Tortillas

It'll all be OK at the corral when you serve up these cheesy bakes

ingredients

1 quantity bolognese sauce (page 26)
8 tortillas or flat breads
1 1/2 cups grated cheddar cheese
chilli sauce, optional

tools

grater
measuring cups
large spoon
baking tray
oven mitts

Make the bolognese sauce (without the spaghetti). Preheat the oven to 180°C (350°F/Gas 4).

Place the tortillas on the work surface and spoon bolognese sauce down the centre of each one. Sprinkle with a little grated cheese and the chilli sauce, if you like it.

Roll up the tortillas to enclose the filling and place them on a baking tray. Sprinkle the tortillas with the rest of the cheese and bake for 15 minutes, or until they are crispy.
Serves 4

Fried Rice

Confucius say "Fried rice is very nice, but sharing it is better"

ingredients

1 cup white rice
1 1/2 cups (12 fl oz) water
1 tablespoon oil
3 spring (green) onions, chopped
2 slices ham, chopped
1 capsicum (pepper), chopped

300 g (10 oz) can corn kernels, drained
3 tablespoons soy sauce
1 tablespoon sweet chilli sauce

tools

measuring jug, cups + spoons
knife + chopping board
can opener
saucepan with lid
frypan
stirring spoon

Place the rice and water in a saucepan over high heat and cook for 10 minutes, or until you can see tunnels in the rice and most of the water has been absorbed. Remove from the heat and put the lid on the pan. Leave for 5 minutes or until tender.

Heat the oil in a large frypan over medium-high heat. Add the onions, ham, capsicum and corn and cook, stirring, for 4 minutes, or until the vegetables are soft.

Add the cooked rice, soy sauce and sweet chilli sauce to the frypan and stir so that the rice is mixed well and heated through.
Serves 4

Creamy Potato Salad

A favourite at BBQs and picnics—you'd better get to it before everyone else does

ingredients

750 g (1 1/2 lb) baby new potatoes
4 rashers bacon, rind removed
1/3 cup mayonnaise
1/3 cup sour cream
1/3 cup chopped chives

tools

knife + chopping board
measuring cups
saucepan
fork
colander

bowl
stirring spoon

Cut the potatoes in half. Cook the potatoes in a large saucepan of boiling water for 7 minutes, or until they are soft when you poke them with a fork. Drain them in a colander and rinse under cold water to cool them.

Cook the bacon under a preheated hot grill (broiler) for 3 minutes each side, or until it is crisp. Let it cool, then break the bacon into small pieces.

Place the mayonnaise, sour cream and chives in a big bowl and mix them together. Add the potatoes and bacon and mix it all together before serving. Serves 4–6

Garlic, Herb & Cheese Breads

Bread needn't be boring—these crunchy rounds are the perfect start to a meal

ingredients

4 long bread rolls or small
   baguettes

garlic butter

2 cloves garlic, crushed

80 g (2 3/4 oz) butter, softened

herb butter

2 teaspoons mixed dried herbs

80 g (2 3/4 oz) butter, softened

cheesy butter

1/2 cup grated cheddar cheese

60 g (2 oz) butter, softened

tools

garlic crusher

3 bowls

measuring cups + spoons

grater

knife + chopping board

aluminium foil

baking tray

oven mitts

Preheat the oven to 180°C (350°F/Gas 4). Slice the bread all the way along, but without cutting all the way through it.

To make the different butters (or just one or two), place the garlic and butter, herbs and butter and cheese and butter in separate bowls and mix well. Spread the butter into the cuts in the bread.

Wrap the bread in aluminium foil and put on a baking tray. Bake in the oven for 15 minutes so that the butter melts and the bread is warm. Serves 4–6

Teriyaki Chicken

Yummy chicken, crunchy vegetables and slippery noodles—this recipe WOKS!

ingredients

2 teaspoons oil
1 onion, chopped
3 chicken breast fillets
1 teaspoon cornflour (cornstarch)
1/3 cup (2 3/4 fl oz) teriyaki sauce

2 carrots, peeled and chopped
1 green capsicum (pepper), chopped
1 tablespoon brown sugar
rice or noodles, to serve
2 tablespoons sesame seeds

tools

measuring jug, cups + spoons
knife + chopping board
vegetable peeler
frypan or wok
stirring spoon + bowl

Heat the oil in a frypan or wok over medium-high heat. Add the onion and stir for 3 minutes, or until it is soft. Slice each chicken fillet into pieces and add to the frypan. Cook the chicken for 4 minutes, or until golden brown.

Put the cornflour and teriyaki sauce in a bowl and mix together so there are no lumps. Add to the frypan with the carrots, capsicum and brown sugar. Cook for 5 minutes, or until the chicken is cooked.

Spoon into serving bowls with rice or noodles. Sprinkle with sesame seeds before serving. Serves 4

Hawaiian Pan Sandwich

Aloha! Treat yourself to a taste of the tropics with these lush sandwiches

ingredients

4 slices bread
butter
2 big slices ham
2 rings canned pineapple
2 big slices cheddar cheese

tools

can opener
butter knife
frypan
spatula or egg flip

Place a frypan over medium heat and wait for it to warm up. While you're waiting, spread both sides of the bread with butter.

Pile 2 slices of the bread with ham, pineapple and cheese. Top with the other 2 slices of bread to make sandwiches.

Place the sandwiches in the pan and cook for 2–3 minutes, or until golden brown and crispy underneath. Turn them over with a spatula and cook for another 2 minutes. Serve them while they are warm and toasty.
Makes 2 sandwiches

Honey & Peanut Lamb Kebabs

Eat these bit by bit off the skewers or by the forkful from a plate

ingredients

300 g (10 oz) lamb, cubed

1 green capsicum (pepper), cubed

1 zucchini (courgette), thickly
   sliced

1 punnet cherry tomatoes

3 tablespoons honey

2 tablespoons peanut butter

1 tablespoon soy sauce

salad, to serve

tools

knife + chopping board

measuring spoons

8 skewers

bowls

pastry brush

Carefully slide a cube of lamb onto a skewer, then a piece of capsicum, zucchini and tomato. Add more pieces (in the same order) until the skewer is full. Do the same with the other skewers.

Mix together the honey, peanut butter and soy sauce and brush over the skewers.

Cook the skewers under a pre-heated hot grill (broiler) for 7 minutes or until the lamb is cooked. As they are cooking, brush them occasionally with the honey mixture. Serve with salad. Makes 8 skewers

Tip For wooden skewers, soak them in water for 20 minutes before you start, to stop them scorching

Stuffed Baked Potatoes

Stuff your baked potatoes so they burst at the seams with tasty toppings

ingredients

4 large potatoes, scrubbed and
  washed

oil, to brush

cheese and bacon filling

1 cup grated cheddar cheese

1/2 cup sour cream or yoghurt

2 rashers bacon, cooked

cheese and avocado filling

1 cup grated cheddar cheese

1/2 cup sour cream or yoghurt

1/2 avocado, chopped

tools

grater

measuring cups

knife + chopping board

baking tray

pastry brush

oven mitts

skewer

Preheat the oven to 200°C (400°F/
Gas 6). Place the potatoes on a
baking tray and brush them with
a little oil. Bake in the oven for
45 minutes, or until they are soft
when you poke them with a skewer.

Prepare the cooked potatoes for
the toppings by cutting a deep
cross in the top of each one.

Spoon the cheese, sour cream
and bacon or the cheese,
sour cream and avocado into
the potatoes. Or make up
your own topping using your
favourite ingredients.
Serves 4

Chop Chop Suey

Try a little kitchen kung-fu and knock up this quick Chinese takeaway favourite

ingredients

2 slices rump steak
1 tablespoon oil
1 onion, chopped
1 capsicum (pepper), chopped
1 carrot, peeled and chopped
2 sticks celery, chopped

200 g (6 1/2 oz) fresh hokkien
   or egg noodles
1 tablespoon cornflour (cornstarch)
3/4 cup (6 fl oz) pineapple juice
3 tablespoons honey
5 tablespoons soy sauce

tools

vegetable peeler
measuring jug, cups + spoons
knife + chopping board
frypan or wok
stirring spoon
bowl

Cut any bits of fat off the steak and then slice the steak. Heat the oil in a large frypan or wok over medium-high heat. Add the onion and stir-fry for 2 minutes, or until soft. Add the steak and stir-fry for 2 minutes, or until brown.

Add the capsicum, carrot, celery and noodles to the frypan and stir-fry for 2 minutes.

Put the cornflour and pineapple juice in a bowl and mix well so there are no lumps. Add the honey and soy and then pour it all into the frypan. Stir-fry for 3 minutes, or until the sauce is thick. Serve in bowls.
Serves 4

Sausage Rolls

Get on a roll and make a batch of these party treats to share around

ingredients

300 g (10 oz) minced (ground) beef
1/4 cup tomato paste
1 egg
1/4 cup dry breadcrumbs
1 sheet ready-rolled puff pastry
milk, to brush
tomato sauce, to serve

tools

measuring cups
bowls
stirring spoon
knife + chopping board
baking tray
pastry brush
oven mitts

Preheat the oven to 200°C (400°F/Gas 6). Put the minced beef, tomato paste, egg and breadcrumbs into a bowl and mix them together. Divide the mixture into 2 piles.

Shape each pile into a sausage as long as the sheet of pastry. Cut the pastry sheet in half and place a sausage down the centre of each piece. Roll the pastry over to cover the sausage. Cut each long sausage roll into thirds.

Place the rolls on a baking tray with the pastry joins underneath, then brush the tops with a little milk. Bake for 20 minutes, or until the pastry is golden. Serve with tomato sauce.
Makes 6

Baked Ham & Egg Rolls

This version of a bread roll is a real handful of flavour

ingredients

2 round bread rolls
2 eggs
1 slice ham, chopped
1/4 cup grated cheddar cheese

tools

knife + chopping board
grater
measuring cups
bowl

fork
baking tray
oven mitts

Preheat the oven to 160°C (315°F/Gas 2–3). Slice the tops from the bread rolls and dig out the fluffy bread inside so that the rolls are hollow.

Put the eggs in a bowl and stir them with a fork. Place the ham and cheese inside the bread rolls, then pour in the egg.

Place the rolls on a baking tray and bake for 25 minutes, or until the filling is golden and set. You can eat the rolls warm or cold.
Serves 2

Roast Chicken Dinner

Not just for Sundays, this is an every-day-of-the-week family favourite

ingredients

1 x 1.6 kg (3 1/4 lb) whole chicken
4 potatoes, peeled and halved
4 wedges pumpkin
4 carrots, peeled
vegetable oil, to brush

tools

vegetable peeler
knife + chopping board
deep baking tray
pastry brush
oven mitts

Preheat the oven to 200°C (400°F/Gas 6). Put the chicken in a deep baking tray and place the potatoes, pumpkin and carrots around it.

Use a pastry brush to lightly brush the chicken and vegetables with oil.

Bake for 1 hour, or until the vegetables are soft and the chicken is cooked through. Remove the chicken from the oven and carve it (you might need to ask an older person to help you). Serve with steamed green beans.
Serves 4–5

Tip To tell when the chicken is cooked, poke it with a skewer and the juices should be clear

Guacamole

Take a quick trip down Mexico way with this fiesta favourite

ingredients

1 avocado
1/2 cup sour cream
2 tablespoons lime or lemon juice
cracked black pepper
chopped chives and chilli sauce,
   optional

corn chips or Gringo's Nachos
   (page 25), to serve

tools

measuring cups + spoons
small sharp knife + chopping board
spoon and fork
bowl

Cut the avocado in half with a sharp knife. Dig a spoon around the seed to lift it out. Spoon the avocado into a bowl and then mash it with a fork.

Add the sour cream, lime juice and pepper to the avocado and mix together.

If you like, sprinkle the guacamole with chives and chilli sauce, then serve with corn chips or Gringo's Nachos.
Serves 4

Celebration Cake

You don't need a special occasion to party on with this perfect passionfruit cake

ingredients

125 g (4 oz) butter
1 cup caster (superfine) sugar
3 eggs
2 cups desiccated coconut
1 cup self-raising flour
1/3 cup sour cream

1 cup thick cream, whipped

passionfruit icing
2 cups icing (confectioner's)
   sugar, sifted
3 tablespoons butter, softened
3 tablespoons passionfruit pulp

tools

measuring jug, cups + spoons
electric mixer + bowl
stirring spoons
20 cm (8 inch) round cake tin
non-stick baking paper
skewer + oven mitts

Preheat the oven to 160°C (315°F/ Gas 2–3). Place the butter and sugar in the bowl of an electric mixer and beat until light and creamy. Add the eggs, one at a time, and beat well. Fold in the coconut, flour and sour cream and mix well.

Line a 20 cm (8 inch) round cake tin with non-stick baking paper. Spoon the mixture into the tin and bake for 45 minutes, or until the cake is cooked in the middle when you poke a skewer into it. Leave the cake until it is completely cold.

For the icing, put the icing sugar, butter and passionfruit pulp in a bowl and mix together. Slice the cake in half and spread the bottom layer with whipped cream. Put the top layer back on and spread with the passionfruit icing.
Serves 8–10

Oaty Scout Cookies

Fund-raising drive or not, these are guaranteed to make you big bickies

ingredients

1 cup rolled oats
1 cup plain (all-purpose) flour
1/2 cup sugar
3/4 cup desiccated coconut
2 tablespoons golden syrup
125 g (4 oz) butter

1/2 teaspoon bicarbonate of soda
1 tablespoon hot water

tools

measuring cups + spoons
bowls
saucepan
stirring spoons
2 baking trays + oven mitts
wire cooling racks

Preheat the oven to 160°C (315°F/ Gas 2–3). Place the oats, flour, sugar and coconut in a large bowl.

Put the golden syrup and butter in a saucepan over low heat and let them melt. Mix the bicarbonate of soda with the water and add to the pan. Pour the butter mixture over the dry ingredients in the bowl and mix together well.

Place flattened tablespoons of the mixture onto baking trays, leaving space between the biscuits so they can spread. Bake for 8–10 minutes, or until golden. Cool on wire racks.
Makes 28

Chocolate Bombs

It's the explosive chocolate flavour that makes these muffins dynamite

ingredients
250 g (8 oz) butter
3 eggs
1 cup caster (superfine) sugar
1 teaspoon vanilla essence
2/3 cup plain (all-purpose) flour
1/3 cup cocoa powder

tools
measuring cups + spoons
saucepan
bowl
stirring spoon
sifter
oven mitts

twelve 1/2-cup (4 fl oz) non-stick
   muffin tins
skewer

Preheat the oven to 180°C (350°F/ Gas 4). Put the butter in a saucepan over low heat and leave to melt. Put the eggs, sugar and vanilla in a bowl and mix well.

Sift the flour and cocoa into the sugar mixture and then add the melted butter and mix well.

Pour the mixture into twelve 1/2-cup (4 fl oz) non-stick muffin tins and bake for 15 minutes, or until the muffins are cooked in the middle when you poke a skewer into them. Cool them in the tins.
Makes 12

Tangy Lemon Spread

This zesty spread is a perfect treat on freshly sliced bread or warm toast

ingredients

90 g (3 oz) butter
1 cup caster (superfine) sugar
1/2 cup (4 fl oz) lemon juice
2 eggs

tools

measuring jug + cups
heatproof bowl
saucepan
stirring spoon
screw-top jar

Place the butter, sugar, lemon juice and eggs in a heatproof bowl and place on top of a saucepan of simmering water.

Stir for 5 minutes, or until the mixture thickens, then remove it from the top of the saucepan— be careful of the steam.

Pour the lemon spread into a clean screw-top jar and keep it in the fridge. It can be spread on toast or sandwiches or over a cake. Makes 2 cups

Tip This spread can be kept in the fridge for up to 4 weeks

Thumbprint Cookies

Go undercover and get your friends' fingerprints on file in these crisp biscuits

ingredients

180 g (6 oz) butter
1 cup caster (superfine) sugar
1 egg
1/2 cup self-raising flour
1 1/4 cups plain (all-purpose) flour
jam or chocolate sweets,
 to decorate

tools

measuring cups + spoons
electric mixer + bowl
stirring spoon
baking tray
non-stick baking paper
oven mitts
wire cooling racks

Preheat the oven to 180°C (350°F/ Gas 4). Place the butter and sugar into the bowl of an electric mixer and beat until light and creamy. Add the egg and beat well. Stir in the flours and mix to a dough.

Line a baking tray with non-stick baking paper. Roll 2 tablespoons of the dough into a ball. Flatten onto the baking tray.

Press your thumb into the middle of the dough to make a hole. Fill the hole with jam or a chocolate sweet. Bake for 10–12 minutes, or until the cookies are golden. Cool on wire racks.
Makes 18

Chockie Moon Rocks

Not quite space food, but definitely an intergalactic taste sensation—and easy!

ingredients

200 g (6 1/2 oz) dark cooking
   chocolate, broken into pieces
1/3 cup shredded coconut
125 g (4 oz) pink and white
   marshmallows, halved

tools

measuring cup
heatproof bowl
saucepan
stirring spoon
2 baking trays

non-stick baking paper

Put the chocolate in a heatproof bowl and place on top of a saucepan of simmering water. Stir until the chocolate is smooth, then remove it from the top of the saucepan—be careful of the steam.

Cool the chocolate slightly and then stir in the coconut and marshmallows. Line 2 baking trays with non-stick baking paper.

Pile spoonfuls of the mixture onto the trays so that they look like rocks. Place the trays in the refrigerator to let the rocks set.
Makes 15

Ultimate Choc-Fudge Sauce

This chocolate sauce is so thick and delicious you'll want to take a dip in it

ingredients

200 g (6 1/2 oz) dark cooking
    chocolate, broken into pieces
1 cup (8 fl oz) cream
ice cream, to serve

tools

measuring jug
saucepan
stirring spoon
bowl
screw-top jar

Put the chocolate and cream in a saucepan over low heat and stir until they make a smooth sauce.

Pour into a bowl and leave it to cool a little.

Pour the warm sauce over ice cream, or pour it into a clean screw-top jar and keep it in the fridge to use cold in a milkshake with loads of ice cream.
Makes 1 1/2 cups.

Tip To reheat the sauce, place it in the microwave for a few seconds

Coconut Macaroons

Having afternoon tea? Pile the plate high with these sweet chewy bickies

ingredients

2 egg whites
1/2 cup sugar
2 cups desiccated coconut

tools

measuring cups + spoons
2 baking trays
non-stick baking paper
bowl
stirring spoon
oven mitts

Preheat the oven to 180°C (350°F/ Gas 4). Line 2 baking trays with non-stick baking paper.

Place the egg whites, sugar and coconut in a bowl and mix together. Press 2 tablespoons of mixture into a ball and put on the baking tray. Do the same with the rest of the mixture.

Bake for 8–10 minutes, or until the macaroons are just starting to brown. Cool on the trays before serving.
Makes 14

Buried Treasure Muffins

Follow this map, me-hearties, to discover the tasty hidden treasure

ingredients

2 cups self-raising flour

1/2 teaspoon ground cinnamon

3/4 cup sugar

300 g (10 oz) sour cream

1 egg

3 tablespoons vegetable oil

3 bananas, roughly mashed

125 g (4 oz) milk chocolate,
　　broken into chunks

tools

measuring cups + spoons

fork

bowls

stirring spoon

twelve 1/2-cup (4 fl oz) muffin tins

skewer + oven mitts

Preheat the oven to 200°C (400°F/ Gas 6). Place the flour, cinnamon and sugar in a bowl and mix. Put the sour cream, egg, oil and bananas in a bowl and whisk together with a fork. Add to the dry ingredients and stir to just combine them.

Spoon the mixture into 12 greased 1/2-cup (4 fl oz) muffin tins until they are half-full. Place a chunk of chocolate on each one and then top with more muffin mixture.

Bake for 25–30 minutes, or until the muffins are golden and cooked in the middle when you poke a skewer into them.
Makes 12 muffins

Giant's Choc-Chip Mega-Cookies

You'll need a crane to crunch into these ginormous chunky choc biscuits

ingredients

125 g (4 oz) butter, softened and chopped

1/2 teaspoon vanilla essence

1 cup brown sugar

1 egg

1 cup plain (all-purpose) flour

1 cup self-raising flour

1 cup desiccated coconut

1 1/2 cups chunks of chocolate

tools

knife + chopping board

measuring cups + spoons

2 baking trays + oven mitts

non-stick baking paper

electric mixer + bowl

wooden spoon

Preheat the oven to 190°C (375°F/ Gas 5). Line 2 baking trays with non-stick baking paper.

Put the butter, vanilla and sugar in the bowl of an electric mixer and beat until creamy. Add the egg and beat for 1 minute. Use a wooden spoon to stir in the flours, coconut and chocolate chunks.

Place a couple of big spoonfuls of mixture on each tray and bake for 20 minutes, or until the cookies are brown. Cool on the trays. The cookies are big so bake them in batches, a couple at a time.
Makes 10 giant cookies

Chocolate Fudge

Chocolate chunks that hundreds and thousands of us love

ingredients

400 g (13 oz) dark or milk
    chocolate, broken into pieces
1 cup (8 fl oz) sweetened
    condensed milk
60 g (2 oz) butter
hundreds and thousands

tools

measuring cup
saucepan
stirring spoon
20 cm (8 inch) square cake tin
aluminium foil
knife

Put the chocolate, condensed milk and butter in a saucepan over low heat and stir until smooth and glossy.

Line a 20 cm (8 inch) square cake tin with aluminium foil and pour the mixture into the tin. Shake hundreds and thousands over the fudge and refrigerate for 2 hours, or until set.

Cut the fudge into small squares to serve or wrap pieces in waxed paper and twist the ends to make a great gift.
Makes 16 squares

Frog in a Pond

Fall hook, line and sinker for a fruity jelly hopping with frogs

ingredients
2 x 85 g (3 oz) packets green
  jelly
4 chocolate or jelly frogs

tools
4 serving glasses
jug

Make the jelly by following the instructions on the packet. Divide the jelly in half and pour one half into a jug and set aside.

Pour the other half of the jelly into 4 wide glasses. Put the glasses in the freezer for 15 minutes, or until the jelly is beginning to set.

Place a chocolate or jelly frog on top of the jelly in each glass, then pour the other half of the jelly over the top. Refrigerate for 30 minutes, or until set.
Makes 4

Chocolate Mousse

Float away with deliciously squishy spoonfuls of this classic chocolate dessert

ingredients

200 g (6 1/2 oz) dark cooking
  chocolate, broken into pieces
45 g (1 1/2 oz) butter
1/2 cup (4 fl oz) cream
4 egg whites
3 tablespoons sugar

tools

measuring cups + spoons
saucepan
stirring spoon
electric mixer + bowl
metal spoon
4 serving glasses

Place the chocolate, butter and cream in a saucepan over very low heat. Stir until the chocolate has melted, then take it off the heat and pour it into a large bowl to cool.

Put the egg whites in the bowl of an electric mixer and beat until light and foamy. Sprinkle with the sugar and beat until the egg white has peaks that stand up— be careful not to overbeat it.

Fold the egg white into the chocolate mixture with a metal spoon, being careful not to stir out the air. Spoon the mousse into glasses and refrigerate until firm. Serves 4

Bumpy Baked Custard

Sweet buried apricots make this dessert a bumpy but blissful ride

ingredients

30 g (1 oz) butter

425 g (14 oz) canned apricot
   halves, drained

2 tablespoons plain (all-purpose)
   flour

3 eggs

3/4 cup (6 fl oz) milk

3/4 cup (6 fl oz) cream

1/3 cup sugar

1 teaspoon vanilla essence

ice cream, to serve

tools

can opener

measuring jug, cups + spoons

saucepan

1-litre (32 fl oz) heatproof dish

blender or food processor

oven mitts

Preheat the oven to 160°C (315°F/ Gas 2–3). Put the butter in a saucepan over low heat and leave to melt. Place the apricot halves, bump side up, in a greased 1-litre (32 fl oz) heatproof dish.

To make the custard, put the flour, eggs, milk, cream, sugar, vanilla and melted butter in a blender or food processor and blend until smooth.

Pour the custard over the apricots and then bake for 30 minutes, or until the custard is firm. Serve in bowls with scoops of ice cream. Serves 4–6

Marble Cake

Three favourite flavours swirl and twirl in one kaleidoscope of a cake

ingredients

250 g (8 oz) butter
1 cup caster (superfine) sugar
1 teaspoon vanilla essence
4 eggs
2 cups self-raising flour
few drops pink food colouring
3 tablespoons cocoa powder

tools

measuring cups + spoons
electric mixer + bowl
wooden spoon
3 bowls
20 cm (8 inch) round cake tin
skewer + oven mitts
wire cooling rack

Preheat the oven to 160°C (315°F/ Gas 2–3). Place the butter and sugar in the bowl of an electric mixer and beat until light and creamy. Add the vanilla and eggs, one at a time, and beat well. Use a wooden spoon to stir in the flour.

Divide the cake mix into 3 bowls. Mix a few drops of pink colouring into one bowl and the cocoa powder into another. Leave one plain. Grease a 20 cm (8 inch) round cake tin and spoon all 3 mixtures into the cake tin.

Use a skewer or knife to swirl the mixtures together to create a marble effect. Bake for 40 minutes, or until the cake is cooked in the middle when you poke a skewer into it. Cool in the tin on a wire rack. Makes 1 big cake

Crazy Cupcakes

Go crazy and colour your cake any way you like it

ingredients

1 1/2 cups self-raising flour
2/3 cup caster (superfine) sugar
125 g (4 oz) butter, softened
3 eggs
1/4 cup (2 fl oz) milk
few drops food colouring
   (any colour)

icing

2 cups icing (confectioner's)
   sugar
3 tablespoons soft butter
2 tablespoons hot water
food colouring (any colour)
sweets or sprinkles, to decorate

tools

measuring cups + spoons
two 12-hole patty cake tins
paper patty cake cases
electric mixer + bowl
spoon
oven mitts
sifter

Preheat the oven to 180°C (350°F/ Gas 4). Line two 12-hole patty cake tins with paper cases. Put the flour, sugar, butter, eggs, milk and food colouring in the bowl of an electric mixer. Beat for 4 minutes, or until the cake mix is smooth.

Spoon the cake mixture into the paper cases until they are three-quarters full. Bake for 18–20 minutes, or until the cupcakes have risen. Remove from the oven to cool.

To make the icing, sift the icing sugar into a bowl and add the butter, hot water and a few drops of food colouring. Mix until smooth. Spread the icing over the cakes and top with sweets or sprinkles. Makes 12

Strawberry & Cream Stars

Aim for the stars with these scrummy jam and cream pastry sandwiches

ingredients

2 sheets ready-rolled puff pastry
1/3 cup jam (any flavour)
1 cup (8 fl oz) thick cream,
   whipped
icing (confectioner's) sugar, to dust

tools

measuring jug + cups
large star cookie cutter
baking tray
non-stick baking paper
oven mitts

knife
sifter

Preheat the oven to 180°C (350°F/Gas 4). Cut stars from the pastry, using a large star cookie cutter. Line a baking tray with non-stick baking paper.

Place the pastry stars on the baking tray. Prick the pastry stars all over with a fork. Bake for 8–10 minutes, or until the stars are puffed and golden. Leave to cool.

Slice the stars in half horizontally and spread the bottom halves with jam and cream. Put the tops back on and sandwich together. Dust with icing sugar before serving. Makes 14 stars

Chocolate No-Bake Slice

No need to get hot under the collar when whipping up these fête favourites

ingredients

180 g (6 oz) sweet biscuits
filling
250 g (8 oz) butter
250 g (8 oz) cream cheese
1 cup caster (superfine) sugar

3/4 cup cocoa powder
200 g (6 1/2 oz) sweet biscuits,
  broken into pieces

tools

measuring cups
23 cm (9 inch) square cake tin
aluminium foil
electric mixer + bowl
wooden spoon + knife

Line the base of a 23 cm (9 inch) square cake tin with aluminium foil. Arrange the biscuits in rows to cover the base of the tin.

To make the filling, place the butter, cream cheese, sugar and cocoa into the bowl of an electric mixer and beat until smooth. Stir in the broken biscuits with a wooden spoon.

Spread the filling over the biscuit base and refrigerate for 2 hours, or until firm. Remove from the tin and cut into slices to serve. Makes 24 slices